MW00423355

To:

From:

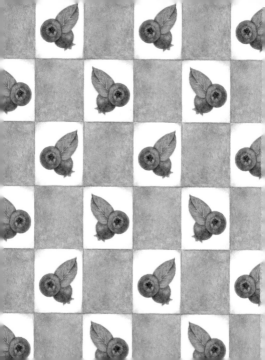

Blueberries from Heaven

A BASKETFUL OF WISDOM

By Carol Tebo

Illustrated by Jo Gershman

INSPIRE

Inspire Books is an imprint of
Peter Pauper Press, Inc.

For permissions, please see the last page of this book.

Designed by Heather Zschock

Text copyright © 2001
Peter Pauper Press, Inc.
202 Mamaroneck Avenue
White Plains, NY 10601
Illustrations copyright © 2001 Jo Gershman
All rights reserved
ISBN 0-88088-143-7
Printed in China
7

Visit us at www.peterpauper.com

Blueberries from Heaven

A BASKETFUL OF WISDOM

Introduction

Most of us can identify an activity which so engrosses our total being that we lose all sense of time. When we are engaged in it, our minds are completely at peace and seemingly devoid of thoughts. At the same time, we are keenly aware of and attuned to our surroundings.

So deeply satisfying is the experience, that for many it takes on an addictive quality.

What these activities have in common is that they are usually solitary, they require sustained physical involvement, and they often take place outdoors and connect us with nature. For some, the activity is gardening. For others, jogging or sailing. For my husband,

it is fishing. For me, it is picking blueberries.

One day while bicycling near our camp in northern New Hampshire, I spied wild blueberries growing along the roadside. Stopping to pick some, I discovered that the field was teeming with the little blue morsels. Blueberry picking became my consuming passion the rest of the summer. It was so

compelling that when I would take
my early morning walk with a
small bucket in hand, intending to
pick "just a few" for breakfast,
invariably I would return home
closer to lunch time. The reverie I
experienced while sitting in the
middle of that field—with the
clouds drifting slowly overhead, the
birds singing and calling, and the
crickets chirping—made it almost

impossible to pull myself away.

After reflecting for some time on my preoccupation with this mesmerizing endeavor, I came to recognize that through my total immersion in the process of blueberry picking, I was making a powerful connection with God and the universe. Little by little, lessons were revealed to me which not only applied to seeking and finding blue-

berries, but to my relationship to life itself. I believe the same connection can be made through other absorbing interests, as well, and that many of the same lessons are waiting to be revealed.

Following are the bits of wisdom I garnered while communing with God in fields of blueberries.

See God's Beauty
in Everything

When I am picking blueberries,
I am focused and in harmony
with my surroundings.
Thus, I experience a heightened

awareness of the beauty in
all Creation. I see it not just in
the majestic mountain peaks,
but in the dew-covered spider's
web, and in the insects buzzing
around my head.

. . . I WILL MEDITATE ON YOUR
WONDERFUL WORKS.

Psalm 145:5 NIV

Often we are juggling so many activities, both physically and mentally, that we are focused on none. Life easily becomes blurred, and we can miss the big picture, as well as the beautiful intricacies in front of us.

When we are anxious, over-whelmed or harried, it is important to stop everything for a moment and direct

our attention: first, to the smallest wonder which catches our eye; then, by slowly expanding our vision in ever-widening circles, to the entire panorama surrounding us.

As we become attuned to the marvels in that very moment, we will gain a fresh perspective on our endeavors. We will see that everything is an integral part of the flow of life. And we will appreciate the wonder of it all.

Be Alert for Opportunities

If I am not vigilant when I walk along the wayside, I may pass by fields full of blueberries and never know they are there.

*I will wonder why I can't find
any, and may falsely conclude
there are none. I must be aware
of the conditions in which blueberries thrive and watchful for
signs that they may be near.*

THEREFORE KEEP WATCH,
BECAUSE YOU DO NOT KNOW
THE DAY OR THE HOUR.

Matthew 25:13 NIV

How many times do we long for positive changes to occur in our lives—a new career, a loving relationship, an exciting adventure? Yet, despite our desire, we often fail to recognize the opportunities that would lead to the fulfillment of our dreams.

"Finding" requires our active participation and attention. We must keep all our senses attuned and be ready to test the possibilities when an opportunity presents itself.

Vigilance is necessary after expressing a need or desire to God, for we do not know by what means or at what time our answer will come. When an opportunity has passed, it cannot be retrieved, and we may then falsely conclude that God hasn't responded to our prayers.

Be Prepared
to Receive

I must always make sure to
have a container handy. No
matter how bountiful a field
I may find, I cannot gather

many blueberries if I am not
prepared. Then I will surely
lament my loss. I must also be
willing to interrupt my plans
and pick berries whenever
I discover a ripe field.

BE DRESSED READY FOR SERVICE AND
KEEP YOUR LAMPS BURNING ...

Luke 12:35 NIV

Without appropriate preparation, it is difficult to achieve our desired goals. For instance, we may want to be great athletes, but without proper physical and mental training, our bodies will not be ready for the contest.

Likewise, we may desire to reap the bounty that God has provided for us. However, we will be unable to gather in our harvest if we do not prepare our minds with right thoughts and attitudes.

We must first believe that we
are worthy, and then approach life
with an attitude of receptivity.
Equally important is our willing-
ness to relinquish our own agendas.
In these conditions, peace and
prosperity will flow naturally
to us.

Listen With Your Soul

When I am quietly picking
blueberries, I can hear the
sounds of silence. They fill me
with peace, joy, comfort, and

reassurance. I hear them with my soul. I also enjoy nature's music and let it speak to me.

MY SOUL WAITS IN SILENCE
FOR GOD ONLY . . .

Psalm 62:1 NASB

It seems we have forgotten how to be quiet, how to listen for the still, small voice within us. Our children no longer lie on their backs and watch the clouds float by, or spend an afternoon observing the workings of an ant colony.

From the sounds of rush hour traffic, the chatter of talk shows, the ba-booming base of the stereo, to the jangle of the telephone, the jarring laugh tracks of TV sitcoms, and the sound effects of computer games, our days and nights are filled with noises—often competing ones.

Little wonder that our nerves are frayed, our serenity demolished, and our psyches fragmented! We use all kinds of drugs to ease the pain, when what we really need is time to just be quiet—to be in the presence of our Creator and Creation, and to listen with our souls.

Look Beneath
the Surface

*Sometimes it appears that there
are very few berries, or none at
all, when I look only at the surface of the plants. But if I kneel*

*down, and gently bend back the
bushes, I will be delighted by
the clusters of plump berries
hidden underneath.*

STOP JUDGING BY MERE
APPEARANCES, AND MAKE
A RIGHT JUDGMENT.

John 7:24 NIV

Whether it is a circumstance, a person, or a relationship, there is always more there than meets the eye. If we look only at the circumstances of a seemingly negative situation, we will misjudge the meaning, or miss the lesson it has to offer.

If we see only the outward appearance of a person, we will lose the oppor-

tunity to know the beautiful soul
that lies within.

And in a relationship, what
may appear to be a breakdown may,
in fact, harbor the seeds of new
understanding if we dig deeper.

To skate along on the surface
of life is merely to exist. What lies
beneath is what gives richness to
our lives and nourishment to our
souls. It is the truth about our
existence, waiting to be discovered.

Believe in God's Infinite Abundance

No matter how many blueberries
I pick, there are always more.
Sometimes, I become anxious
when I see someone else picking
in "my" field, fearing that

I won't get all I need.
Then I realize that no one can
ever pick them all. God has
provided enough for each of us,
and I need never worry.

. . . DO NOT BE ANXIOUS ABOUT YOUR
LIFE . . . IT IS YOUR FATHER'S GOOD
PLEASURE TO GIVE YOU THE KINGDOM.

Luke 12:22, 32 RSV

As a hamster stuffs its pouches, we humans often hoard our possessions, clutching them tightly to our breasts.

Yet, possessing is illusory, at best. Ask anyone whose belongings have been taken in a fire or by a tornado. And also ask them to tell you how the Universe responds with unimagined generosity, quickly filling the seeming void.

When Jesus fed the multitudes,

he looked beyond the appearance
of the meager supplies at hand, and
thanked God for the abundance he
knew was there.

We, also, must approach life
with the same attitude of thankful-
ness and receptivity. Then it is easy
to see that God has created a world
in which there is enough for all.

See With
New Eyes

When I walk along a roadside
picking all the blueberries I see,
I am always amazed to find
more as I walk back in the

*opposite direction. They were
there all the time. How could
I have missed them?*

...UNLESS ONE IS BORN ANEW,
HE CANNOT SEE
THE KINGDOM OF GOD.

John 3:3 RSV

Until we change direction, we see things from only one perspective—and the chances are good that there is much we are missing.

Most life-changing inventions and discoveries are made because someone dares to look at the world in a new way. What advances would have been missed

had we continued seeing the world as flat, man as

earthbound, penicillin as mold, matter as inert?

Likewise, we limit our understanding of life when we view it only from the perspective of our five senses. Until we shed our self-imposed restrictions, freeing ourselves to experience the intangible aspects of existence, we cannot accept the life of the Spirit that lies within us. When we do, we will behold the Kingdom of God!

Recognize True Worth

It came to me one day,
as I was searching for the
biggest blueberries, that small
berries would fill my cup just

as surely as large ones.
And, often, they were sweeter.

...THIS POOR WIDOW HAS
PUT MORE INTO THE TREASURY
THAN ALL THE OTHERS.

Mark 12:43 NIV

We have all dreamed about doing something grandiose, of "making our mark on the world." However, at some time in our life's journey, we may have to re-evaluate how we measure our worth.

Not all of us are destined for greatness as the world defines it. Our greatness might be seen only when we step back and view the beautiful collage created by the blending of our many small deeds

and accomplishments.
No single one may stand
out, yet without it, the
world would be just a bit different.

It is often the little gift or small
meaningful gesture which most
tenderly touches the heart. Each act
of love, no matter how tiny, sends
out a mighty ripple across the
Universe. When we give what we
have in love, we indeed leave our
mark on the world!

Exercise
Discernment

If I try to pick blueberries before
they are ripe, I must tug and
pull. And even if I'm successful,
they don't taste good. If I wait

too long, they become over-ripe,
and fall to the ground and are
lost. For the greatest reward,
I must pick them at their
peak of readiness.

BUT WHEN THE GRAIN IS RIPE,
AT ONCE HE PUTS IN THE SICKLE,
BECAUSE THE HARVEST HAS COME.

Mark 4:29 RSV

H uman beings are much like fruit. They mature slowly and in their right time, requiring tender care and love to ripen fully.

If we attempt to force people to mature faster or before they are ready, they will cling tenaciously to what is familiar and resist our efforts. The best thing we can do is pray and wait.

Sometimes, a person may try to make external changes before being motivated from within. Often such changes last only a short while, because they are not authentic.

When people's souls have ripened, it is important for us to recognize their readiness and receive their gifts with open arms. If we fail to do so, their fruit may wither and be lost.

Be Patient

Some years I am disappointed
to find that the blueberry crop is
very sparse. The next season,
I rejoice that it is exceedingly
abundant. I realize that the

bushes were resting so they could bear fruit with increased vigor.

… THEY THAT WAIT UPON
THE LORD SHALL RENEW
THEIR STRENGTH …

Isaiah 40:31 KJV

Waiting is one of the most difficult things for a child. Time seems to stand still when anticipating a special event.

Come to think of it, waiting is difficult for adults, too! TV advertisements continually prod us to "HURRY! Get it NOW!" We expect things to happen quickly, and we are disappointed when they don't.

Too often we try to run out ahead of life, instead of meeting it

as it greets us each day.
Because of our impatience,
we experience fruitless worry and
frustration.

Many times, in retrospect, we
are able to see why waiting was
necessary; that a greater good than
we had envisioned was the result.
Then, our faith is strengthened and
our spirits lifted as we learn to wait
with anticipation, rather than
impatience, upon the Lord.

Welcome Adversity

*It is easy to gather blueberries
when they are plentiful,
but if I persevere I can obtain
what I need even in years
when there are very few. I derive*

deep satisfaction when I produce jam* from berries I have worked hard to collect.

. . . WE ALSO REJOICE IN OUR
SUFFERINGS, BECAUSE WE KNOW THAT
SUFFERING PRODUCES PERSEVERANCE;
PERSEVERANCE, CHARACTER;
AND CHARACTER, HOPE.

Romans 5:3-4 NIV

* *Spicy Blueberry Jam recipe is at the end of the book.*

Many people are addicted to having things easy and convenient. They complain the minute life becomes the least bit difficult, and shy away from tasks they cannot accomplish quickly and readily.

Such people never test the limits of their endurance and, therefore, never discover the heights to which they might soar. They are but hollow images of their true selves.

Others who have endured pain,

suffering, and hardship often are aglow with peace and joy. One might ask how that can be. It is because their overcoming of adversity has strengthened their character and produced an unshakable hope and confidence in the undergirding goodness and love of God. They have the satisfaction of knowing they have stood the test.

Cherish Each Individual

I have witnessed myself, and others, doing a very curious thing. No matter how many blueberries I already have, if I

drop one, I will dig around in
the brush until I find it. Each
berry is a treasure like no other.

. . . REJOICE WITH ME;
I HAVE FOUND MY LOST SHEEP.

Luke 15:6 NIV

There are many ways that our society tells us that the beautiful, rich, and famous are somehow more important than we are. In addition to receiving exorbitant salaries, their activities are portrayed in the media—as though their lives have more significance than ours.

Yet, in the overarching scheme of the Universe, these "super humans" are no more indispensable than you or I. One star does not light up the sky!

It is always a moving reminder to participate in a candlelight service. The darkened room gradually becomes ablaze with light as each person blends his individual flame with the next, creating a powerful awareness that each one of us is an essential part of the whole of Creation. Without our special light, the world is a little less bright. That is how important we are!

Accept God's Timing

It is good that I can't pick
blueberries all year round.
I would not get anything else
done. And, I would not be

*able to experience the joy
of anticipation as summer
approaches.*

To every thing there is a season,
and a time to every purpose
under the heaven...

Ecclesiastes 3:1 KJV

Sometimes it is difficult to accept the rhythms and seasons of life. Modern technology has made it possible for us to bypass most of nature's vicissitudes. Heating keeps us warm; air conditioning keeps us cool; plows remove the snow; reservoirs collect

the rain—and so we are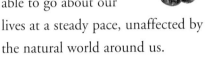
able to go about our
lives at a steady pace, unaffected by
the natural world around us.

This creates a false illusion that
we are in control of life. We try to
hurry through winter to spring; to
rush out of the valley and up to
the mountain top; to make the
dark turn instantly to light. We
continually resist letting life unfold
naturally. Consequently, our lives

are terribly out of kilter.

With maturity comes the understanding that waiting is just as fruitful as charging ahead; resting is as important as acting; darkness is as necessary as light; and an occasional snow day is good for both body and soul. The ebbs and flows of life are essential. Our renewal and growth depend upon them.

Rejoice in Diversity

Blueberries are delicious all by themselves. I can savor their texture and taste. They also contribute their unique flavor to other ingredients to make

muffins, pies, or jam. They are
especially good when they are
fresh, but freezing them allows
me to enjoy them later.
Blueberries are special,
no matter how I use them.

THERE ARE DIFFERENT KINDS
OF GIFTS, BUT THE SAME SPIRIT.

1 Corinthians 12:4 NIV

It is a natural tendency to gravitate toward, and feel kindred to, those who think, feel and enjoy what we do. For some purposes, this serves us well—such as sharing a hobby.

However, it is the differences of others which most often contribute to our growth by introducing us to new ideas and stimulating us to see the world from other perspectives. Combining our differences enables us to accomplish so much more than we could on our own.

We often unconsciously seek out a person different from ourselves with whom to share an intimate relationship because something in us recognizes that our strengths and weaknesses need to be complemented and balanced.

It is important to know that each of us was designed to play a unique role in life and to add our own special flavor.

Share God's Gifts

*I feel so blessed by God's
gift of blueberries. But it makes
me feel especially good when
I share it with others.*

IT IS MORE BLESSED TO GIVE
THAN TO RECEIVE.

Acts 20:35 NIV

At some time we have all
watched a good movie,
attended an exciting football
game, participated in an enlight-
ening conversation, or strolled
through a beautiful woods—only
to find our enjoyment dampened
because someone we cared about
was not there to
share it. We knew it
would be impossible
to convey to that

person second-hand the special
feelings of that moment.

God created life in pairs
because he planned it to be
shared. Sharing eases the pain of
difficult times and makes the joy
of good times sweeter.

God's bounty was also intended to be shared. Our possessions, in themselves, do not have the ability to make us happy. Many millionaires have come to that realization late in life, and have found redemption only in sharing their

fortunes with others.

Sharing ourselves
and our abundance
opens our hearts and reminds us of
our interdependence. The gift we
give blesses us in return.

Life Never Ends

I felt great anxiety when my
favorite blueberry field was
mowed in the fall. I was sure
the blueberry plants were dead
and gone forever. But the next

summer, there they were—thou-
sands of tiny blue testimonies
to the regenerating force of life!

THY KINGDOM IS AN EVERLASTING
KINGDOM, AND… ENDURETH
THROUGHOUT ALL GENERATIONS.

Psalm 145:13 KJV

I n so many ways life tries to
show us that it is everlasting
and connected.

We see it in the looks and
mannerisms of a child who so
strongly resembles a grandparent.

We trace it in the bloodline of
a race horse or a pedigreed dog.

We observe it
when a wound heals,
when new hair
comes back after

radiation treatments, and when a stroke victim's brain regenerates pathways.

We rejoice in it each spring, when the frozen earth gives way to new shoots of grass, the barren trees turn yellow-green with emerging leaves, and dormant bulbs produce bright daffodils and tulips.

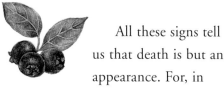

All these signs tell us that death is but an appearance. For, in truth, life never really ends.

The hours I spent in the blueberry fields allowed me to be transported from the bondage of the external world for a while, and allowed God to fulfill His covenant in me:

I WILL PUT MY LAWS
IN THEIR MINDS AND WRITE
THEM ON THEIR HEARTS.

Hebrews 8:10 NIV

Spicy Blueberry Jam

8 cups blueberries (I use wild ones)
2 tablespoons apple cider vinegar
5 cups sugar
1/2 teaspoon salt
1/2 teaspoon each ground cinnamon
   and cloves

Wash and drain berries. Mash about 1 cup
berries to provide juices to start cooking.
Put all berries into kettle and boil about
5 minutes. Add other ingredients and boil
rapidly almost to the jellying point. Skim
and pour boiling hot jam into hot (boiled)
jelly jars. Seal at once with canning lids.
Turn upside down on towel to cool.
Store in refrigerator.

Makes 24 ounces.

Scriptural References

Scripture quotations marked NASB are taken from the *New American Standard Bible*. Copyright © 1960, 1962, 1963, 1968, 1971, 1972, 1973, 1975, 1977 by The Lockman Foundation. Used by permission.

Scripture quotations marked NIV are taken from the *Holy Bible, New International Version*®. Copyright © 1973, 1978, 1984 by International Bible Society. Used by permission of Zondervan Publishing House. All rights reserved.

Scripture quotations marked KJV are taken from the *King James Version* of the Bible.

Scriptures marked RSV are taken from the *Revised Standard Version* of the Bible, Copyright © 1946, 1952, and 1971 by the Division of Christian Education of the National Council of the Churches of Christ in the U.S.A. Used by permission. All rights reserved.

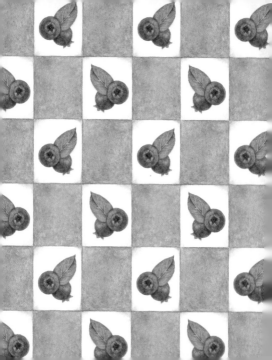